# Mood and Dream

*

## essay

*

## Traumear

*

Mood and dream foreshadow the ideal effectiveness of our soul on behalf of ourselves and others. They indicate for us, each in its own way, that an operational soul is available for us and places in our hands the means whereby we may arrive at, or attain to, this greatest of all benefits within reach of every human being. It makes sense that once we have worked our way through this possibility a few times, we will be much less afraid of, and less vulnerable in the presence of, depressions and elations in ourselves and others, while images and symbols, as we accidentally produce them ourselves and as they crop up like weeds all around us, will cause us less anxiety and tempt us less frequently.

(from page 40)

\*

iv

# Mood and Dream

Mood is a word with not much currency of its own. Neither is dream. We talk about mood music, about a dream sequence. Beyond that we usually mean moods and dreams.

I have a special reason for linking mood and dream. Religion depends on both. We become separated from our human nature. We notice this and quickly move to repair the damage. That is a religious move. Mood and dream aid us, in different, almost in apposite ways.

Moods and dreams happen to us but mood is there to be identified and dream is here to be sourced. The identification of mood lends us objectivity for a time. We have something to work with, to push against, something that affords us leverage during a massive struggle. Mood is like a build-up of energy then for which we have neither reason nor excuse. We feel it however, in general as a burden, as a pressure – as depression.

This is before we say – or others say – that we are moody or in a mood. The burden of mood, the mood burden, is raw experience and it calls for a tactic. We are not burdened because we were bad or because our parents, our forebears, were bad but so that we may find a tactical response in terms of that rarity called human nature.

Dream, by comparison, is the source that makes out for us a creative subjectivity of sorts. Dream exists only because we rely on it – if and when we rely on it, otherwise it does not exist and it would be nonsensical to insist that it does.

Dream could also be called the work principle. The urge to work is one thing and dream is another, while together they come into being a human/divine creation.

The objectivity of mood and the subjectivity of dream may be independently pursued but their contemporary communion works wonders. We need to take a close look at that before we can identify within ourselves certain relevant organic processes that depend, for their existence, as much on our timely recognition of them, as upon a human-natural dynamic of their own.

*

We can identify mood in ourselves simply by giving in to the *exigencies of the moment*. Here we are, at this particular time for example and our personal contact with our environment is not initiated by us. We might be able to help or hinder it but we choose not to. This is when mood feeling, or mood experience, comes to the fore. We do not try to meditate it away, buddhistically, but we bear it; we bear up under it. Of course we have our reasons for doing so. What might they be?

Think of it as an offering of life. You are willing to offer life to others, to those, perhaps, who have none but mostly to those who have and wish for more. Call it cross-fertilization. Life you offer to another is life you gain. That, in short, is the law. We do well to keep it in mind, lest we reach for life, hoping in vain to appropriate it.

Giving in to the *exigencies of the moment* – that is easily enough said. We are trained from childhood and schooled from adolescence to defend ourselves against those very *exigencies*, to disown them, to shake them off. We practice something we call will power in order to escape from any claim they appear to make on us. Giving in to them we suffer. Our whole being bristles.

Mood can never be a social entity. We dare not admit to one another the presence of mood and much prefer to pretend that no mood exists, that we are beyond it. Our pride is involved. Why should we be ashamed of mood in our presence? It lingers and we feel depressed by it. It is the depression. Perhaps we long for, reach for, an anti-depressant drug. Certainly a stimulant seems called for. Our problem is, we are not happy. Society dictates lip service to happiness. I in your society would not 'let you down' by exposing you to mood, to my mood, to my moodiness. Of course we may be friends, then that is a different story. We may even become friends by allowing for each other's mood. More of that later. For the moment let us concentrate on the *exigencies of the moment* as harbingers of mood.

Personality dispels mood. However this must be understood aright. As a person, and as I choose to be personal, I give in to your, not to my, exigencies of the moment. No trickery is involved. I suffer your mood. You may not even notice but that is not important. An unfailing sensibility teaches me how to suffer your mood, your depression – or your elation.

Yes, depression is only one side of mood. Elation is the other. Not to worry, they are both identifiable by similar criteria. Would we not rather be elated than depressed? Our social status is involved, otherwise we would behave similarly towards both.

*

A telling circumstance, this, that we would rather be elated than depressed. It tells us this and that about ourselves. This is our wish to be happy. That is our dogged insistence that no one shall remind us of our liability to unhappiness. So we ignore something rather crucial here, namely that depression and elation both happen. We ourselves are left out of it inasmuch as intention is concerned. We can no more intend to be elated than we can intend to be depressed. It comes about; they both do, usually in turns.

That is mood. Depression is mood and elation is mood. We do well to respect that. Don't confuse it with a bad mood and a good mood, that comes later, as we shall see. At this stage we want to be sure that we recognize 'mood as such', which is depression or elation, which happens or comes about, there we are, stuck with it for the moment, so it seems, and blissfully acting it out.

3

No, we are not acting it out, that is precisely what we have to be honest enough to admit. It is acting us out.

We can see right away when someone is depressed or elated but only if they have given in to it. Therein lies the great curiosity of mood. It happens to us, out of the blue, and then we either drift along with it, unconsciously, like flotsam, or we become conscious of it. That spark of consciousness may suddenly be lit for us and then we know, with a peculiar knowledge we call consciousness, that we are elated or depressed. Consciousness begins there. Mood begins earlier, we should think about that, reflect on it.

It is in fact consciousness that allows us to say, and promptly: mood is earlier. It must have been earlier. Then we see it in some of those around us too, this unconscious mood, and we become a bit contemptuous, forgetting or not honestly realizing that we ourselves had precious little to do with the lighting of that spark of consciousness in ourselves. What a blessing it was, really, come to think of it like 'rain out of the blue'!

Is this when we begin to compare ourselves? Of course it is. Look, there, the unconscious masses, depressed one minute, elated the next, tossed back and forth by chance, tumbling from horrid war into unbearable peace and back into war again, in the family, the neighbourhood, the global conflation of states. It's the *enantiodromia* of Heraclitus, which he recognized even then, ever so long ago and yet, in another and perhaps more reasonable sense, just the other day.

Is it any wonder that the consciousness sets off a bout of contempt? How could it be otherwise? Well, perhaps it could, we know of no law that says it couldn't. We only see what is usually the case, in ourselves and all around. A little education into consciousness produces the prig, the snob, the superior being; the Übermensch.

There's no justification, mind you, for slapping ourselves on the back as if we had merited. There was the depression and the elation and lo, there followed the consciousness, so that the little lord might compare himself to his unconscious brethren and look down on them. He can boss them about now, bully them, lead them – by the nose, usually. He becomes the aristocrat and quite likes himself in that role. Does it occur to him that he has not merited consciousness? Perhaps it does, but that still leaves him at liberty to contemplate himself as 'the lucky one', the one chosen by the gods, to press the yoke onto the shoulders of the unconscious masses. The history books leave us in no doubt as to what goes on and why it goes on and the daily news sheet continues where they leave off. What a spectacle! Most instructive. Of course we do it ourselves from time to time, when we flaunt our bit of learning and feel a sort of delicious superiority for those who 'haven't got it'. But it is sad.

Mood happens to us. Consciousness happens too and when it does we may know that mood has preceded. We feel the pressure and we say: 'Oh, I do need a lift'. We make ourselves a cup of coffee or go to a football match or a performance of Mahler's fifth symphony; or we invade a country; that too gives a body a lift. What an elation, to "ride in triumph"! We may get the stuffing knocked out of us, which can be depressing for a time.

So consciousness brings with it, as we notice, the liberty to manipulate our mood – and then we have moods. As a phenomenon this is most absorbing for the intellect. When we're down and if we find that unpleasant, we can do something, for once. We can make ourselves come up. We bully the wife or the husband, we rub it in that we have what he or she doesn't and that produces a definite change, in the direction of anti-depression. Then we're in a good mood. We have succeeded in impressing our ego upon some poor, unsuspecting individual, or scores of individuals (as in politics) and this is bound to put us in a good mood. If we get slapped down, what then? Why, we're in a bad mood. It's a bad mood if our anti-depressant manipulation has failed.

We still move about on the shadow side of life here. Eventually we will emerge into the light. Right now I want to be quite sure to secure this point of the difference between mood and moods. Mood is never good or bad. It's quite out of the question. Mood is not conscious. I don't expect you to accept this if consciousness has not yet happened to you but if it hasn't, would you still be with me? Hardly.

So in myself I knew nothing about my mood life or mood nature prior to the advent of consciousness. Then, in retrospect, and also in view of my ability to have an effect on my depression and elation, I came to the conclusion that such mood status is objectively available to me, for instance by way of consciousness.

Technically I don't have to wait until mood is depressive or elative. Certainly I don't have to sit back or stand by until I am in a good or a bad mood before I acknowledge this availability to me of objective mood.

However, before we go into this intentional approach to objective mood we should just make sure that we don't make too much of a schematic thing out of the progression from unconscious to conscious mood. Consciousness is not a light which stays on once it is switched on, by who knows what. Every day it happens that we drift along for a bit, unthinking and unfeeling, absent minded, forgetful of who, what and where we are. We get jogged into consciousness then, from within or without, and then we know, hopefully because we have learned, that the mood life or mood nature is there, is available. Why is that so important, that we have learned that and can call it to mind at crucial wake-up moments?

It's important because we don't want to get into the bad habit of depending on good moods. In fact, if we have to an extent indulged in mood manipulation, which is rather likely in modern surroundings, we do well to get away from that, to wean ourselves off it. Have nothing to do with good or bad moods and just plain manage to leave them and all dependence on them to one side by concentrating on mood awareness.

*

We become capable of mood awareness as soon as we understand how readily we are swayed to indulge in conscious manipulation of those states of depression and elation because then we return to mood as such, objective mood – in the interest of what? Why bother. Why not carry on attempting to oppose depression and to sustain elation? In other words, why not continue to pursue happiness?

I suppose the simplest answer is: Because it achieves nothing and wears a fellow out. There are no lasting results. There is no permanent pay-off.

Awareness of mood as such takes care of any depression or elation. The pressure we initially felt or experienced and the elation which amounted to heedlessness – we no longer react against them or fall in which them but we undercut them, so to speak, because we know now about mood. Time and again will arise that temptation, in line with consciousness, to manipulate, to invent devices and to discover mechanisms which will allow us at least to minimize the pressure, by way of anti-depressants, and to prolong the elation, euphorically, as if weightlessness were a solution to pain.

Still, it's this 'running back and forth', this *enantiodromia*, that gives rise to consciousness in the first place, which is like an awakening out of a stupor. We are being shaken and we turn over in our sleep, this way and that way, half awake then drowsing again before the next impulse of pain. At this stage we know nothing about mood, we are only in a mood, a good one or a bad one, as we get into the habit of saying, complacently or plaintively. And we tend to lord it over those who are less conscious, those who are entrapped by some elation, perhaps underpinned by zealotry and those who are burdened by some depression, perhaps aggravated by ignorant behaviour. We tend to lord it over them as we glory in our consciousness and seek to identify it. We seek might and then more might. Some call it power but it's might all the same. It springs from what we consciously make. There is no awareness as yet. We know nothing of it. We are too much enamoured by the pictured possibilities that lead us astray. More might is what we seek and we hope to achieve it by intensifying consciousness as we become technologically more capable, more defensive and aggressive, more proud of ourselves as successful manipulators of fate.

Along with unavoidable failure comes despair and in our despair it may occur to us to accredit mood as such, which is the beginning of true understanding and deserves to be called conscience. Mood is the gift, the presence of our soul, if you like, and we cannot take any credit for it. We cannot 'make it happen'. It is there all the same, objectively. The conscience we may come up with and which may occur to us could be called the path to awareness or the path of awareness. Instead of running back and forth brandishing our mighty tools and instruments we walk, for the first time perhaps, cooperatively with that which we cannot control but it exists in our favour. Thought a feeling come together. Conception and passion are no longer separate; we realize that they have never been separate except to our merely conscious point of view.

The fact that mood is there, objectively, cannot be appreciated except conscientiously. The merely conscious individual cannot 'make anything of it' and therefore it does not exist for him. He cannot make anything of it to boost his ego; he mistakes ego-energy for life and worships it intensely.

8

Conscience is understanding of mood as unmalipulable and as gratuitously favourable. Awareness informs us of the truth of mood and allows us to become truthful. Out of this truthfulness then grows our ethical behaviour, when we decide to do good because that empowers us and power is the ability to do good and the capacity for it.

*

How is mood 'there, objectively'? It seems like a thing to say solely to attract attention. Can you point at mood? Can you point it out to someone?

Well, spiritually and inwardly, there it is, that's clear. I only need to look for it and there it is. However when I say it is there objectively then I mean on one hand that my looking for it, my seeking it, has to do with it being there and on the other hand that it makes no sense to say it is there if I do not look for it. Does that make it merely a projection of my self?

Not at all. First of all, a project is not an object. I project into nothing and nowhere but I object to something. That to which I object in the case of mood is my soul, interestingly enough. It is my soul as mere and pure speculation to which I object. And that objection draws it into the realm of the substantial. I am not, at bottom, content with my soul as a matter of hear-say, as 're-ceived wisdom'. It was not that when I was a child and I refuse to have it as that any longer now. I look for my substantial soul and this 'look', this search, implies coincidentally an objection to my soul as a dogmatic construct. I would even say that it amounts to the same if I object to a supposed absence of soul in myself, or to a trivialization of it. I look and I will not believe that it will not reveal itself to me. I search for that which cannot possibly not be there and I strongly object to all so-called evidence of it not being there. Then there it is, objectively. That is mood. It was there when I was a child and I took it for granted. What do you expect? Of course I did. So did you. Years of strife and struggle intervened. Consciousness intervened. Ma-

9

ture vision, affected by and directed towards environment and community, insists on contemporary terminology, which recaptures the primitive stake we have in our childhood and adapts it to the world in which we live without being mixed up in it. *Enantiodromia* leads to consciousness, leads to conscience, leads to awareness.

Objective mood-awareness is substance, is foundation. There it is, you need no longer quarrel with your fate or long for happiness. Happy are you who look for your soul and find it. When you have it as mood you have cause to be content. You have testimony now, you are no longer speaking merely from yourself. You have the witness that counts. Go ahead and speak now. Let your voice be heard.

*

Bearing up under the *exigencies of the moment*, giving in to them – suffering. Oh how we hate to suffer! We are willing to put up with all sorts of moods just so that we don't have to suffer. And of course we confuse suffering with pain. But here is the strange thing: We are in pain because we did not suffer and because we do not suffer. We do not let our nature deal with the *exigencies of the moment*, with the *striations of time*. Why do we have it backwards? Why does it hurt to do so? Why the horror in the face of that which would prepare us for life?

We do not know that that is what it is. We do not recognize it. Instead we panic. Our senses are revolted. Fear takes us by the throat and squeezes the remaining bit of life out of us.

It is so difficult to believe that our nature can cope with realty, that we do not have to protect it? We shelter behind all these purpose-built safety features and knock ourselves out trying to maintain them when all along nothing is required except faith in our human nature, in what we were born with. The vilification of human nature need not concern us. Why bother describing it? Criticism enhances the problem we wish to be rid of. Do not even hinder the intellectual, the individual, the critic. Learn to believe that the sunlight and the rain are here for you. The light of day draws attention to your human natural requirements and you may search in ourself not only for your own solutions but for mine too.

Suffering, enduring, bearing – I can't bear it, we say. I cannot bear it any longer. I refuse to put up with it any longer. I have come to the end of my tether. – Why are you tethered in the first place? All that pain, as it accumulates, surely it testifies to our persistent refusal to suffer, to let our human nature cope, to let healing take place. Let it take pride of place. Get out of the way. Remove your self from the premises just for once and see how expertly the doctor within you treats you.

Does that mean you should become less aware? On the contrary. Trust and awareness increase simultaneously. Suddenly you find yourself in one mood or another. You are downcast, cranky, sullen. You are indignant, outraged, resentful. Those are all 'bad moods'. Or you are euphoric, triumphant, gleeful, you are in high spirits, walking on air, heedlessly cheerful. Those are 'good moods'. All moods, good or bad, amount to the same. High spirit or low spirits, depression or elation, under pressure or without foundation, happy or unhappy – if you can take the leap to awareness, fine and dandy. You may have to become conscious first, to 'wag the dog', to search for that 'self-licking ice cream cone'. For how long will that have to go on? No one can say. Really it's up to you. Consciousness makes up your mind towards arrogance or conscience. You may get into the way of feeling ever so proud of your conscious ability to manipulate your moods. At the same time of course you may try to manipulate and control the moods of others. You will try to argue them out of their bad moods or you will punish them for being happy when you are down in the mouth. But nothing holds for long. You are bored. The *exigencies of the day* bore into you but you refuse to bear them – so you are surrounded by refuse.

11

You cry out for change. Any change is bound to be good. You find yourself a hero and shout his slogans. The world is full of those who want to change the world, they get all excited, but don't expect global agreement. World war gives way to cold war gives way to terrorism. The socialists are in power, then the conservatives, then the liberals. It's not power but might they seek and when they have it, they bully and screw the lid down on the coffin. Your individual at liberty may come up with conscience but then again he may not. More liberty does not guarantee more conscience, more searching for value and truth. Conscience is just as possible in the penitentiary.

But beware of 'a conscience'! It gets used to manipulate moods. A conscience is a facile tool in the hands of the hypo-crite. When the spark of consciousness is locked up in a box it turns into a conscience. There are those who will do it for you, expertly, professionally, officially, in orthodox fashion and per-fectly organized. These kind guardians will protect you against awareness. They will do that for you with incense and propa-ganda. Just don't mistake your hyperconsciousness for aware-ness, because then you deserve the incense and the propaganda. I wonder what is worse, a lack of conscience or a conscience. Let's all be hypocrites – actors, pretenders, posers. It takes a conscience, a good one or a bad one. Our conscience will re-flect our moods, good or bad. We will avoid the crisis of awareness. What crisis? Oh, the realization that we have been, and are still, wasting our own and everyone else's time with our superior consciousness. How can we continue to lord it over others unless we develop a conscience in terms of how good it must be for them that we do so? Let's turn it into 'a man's world' and into 'a woman's society'. That way the male and the female can co-exist without getting too much into each other's hair, although accidents will happen, otherwise the race would die out. Let's be clinical-cynical, for once. I rely on mood to see me through. The objective reality of my soul is being tested. Am I to hide behind the skirts of my conscience? Let me be conscientious instead. It does take courage.

Once we become aware of the danger of hypocrisy, we are bound to go through a period of cleansing the temple. I have harboured the money changers in my body so now let me get rid of them. Conscience drives me. I do not object to being driven.

*

Let healing take place; be aware objectively of your soul as mood. Again and again you will be in a mood and you may take it as an opportunity for healing, for once again becoming whole. We as human beings do our best work when we are whole. Time and again we sustain an injury. Besides, how can we help those who as yet are not aware, or no longer aware, of their nature in the round if we do not allow ourselves to be moved by their predicament? We enter into their prison and we are not afraid to do so because we know how to leave that prison, leading them out.

My soul is inward reality but awareness, by definition, is of both inward and outward reality. Universal spirit, the father spirit, creative spirit issues within me as my soul and while I am aware of it, this spirit is able to manifest itself outwardly. In that sense now my awareness is the bridge that makes healing available to others. This is how awareness must be understood, as the connection of the inward with the outward reality. At the same time that which is within me and real cannot be wholly real for me until I lead it out to benefit you and others. I become whole myself by helping you to become whole. The healer is not unwilling to be infected from without because he knows how to cure from within.

Contemporary art, by the same token, is not an art of consciousness nor of heightened consciousness but of conscience and awareness. The reality, the true reality within the art worker, becomes real for him even as he allows it to become real out-

13

wardly too. Faith in his sound human nature allows his soul to become cooperative as mood. What he makes out here does not merely carry the imprint of what he is in here but what he creates out here is revealed as real on account of its conjunction with what is real in here. In that way contemporary art especially creates awareness. It places the capacity for wholeness into the hands of the one who would be whole and healed. True genius is always contemporary.

*

What is the 'unfailing sensibility' that teaches us to suffer one another's mood, one another's depression and elation? Is it not all too obvious how in society, however we really are at the moment, we feel obliged to please, to appear pleasant? Is that not what it means to be civil and polite? Surely that is just one, and not the least telling, of the several parts of the social contract, that we conceal our unpleasantness and appear to be pleasant; in short that we appear to be happy. We want to be liked and we know that no one likes an unhappy person. We want to be happy, so let us please be surrounded by happy persons. Like attracts like. You meet me and ask: 'How are you?' The thing for me to say is: 'Fine,' or 'Very well, thank you'. No actual or real state of affairs has anything to do with it. I may let my depression peep through and say: 'Not too bad,' but I must say it cheerfully. What if I answered: 'I am depressed'? Would you not run a mile?

Well, that depends on who you are, on how you yourself are at that moment, on whether we are married, acquainted, companions, friends or perhaps total strangers. It depends on the *exigencies of the time.* That first greeting, more often than not, is but an introduction, which then allows us to feel one another out. Are we at that moment capable or willing to do more than exercise a social amenity or two? We may be so busy and preoccupied within ourselves that it would be quite wrong to do more than just glance off one another. Let the social amenities

14

therefore be nothing more than an important expedient, for letting us get on with what is more important for us at that time – which may of course be a mere genuine acknowledgment of one another. Or you wish to chat but I want to get to the library but, because we have met, a sort of mix occurs, a communal moment, let us call it. Innumerable possibilities arise. We may end up chatting or you may accompany me to the library. We may decide to have lunch at a restaurant and eventually get married, who can say. Meetings are fraught with possibility, rich in living potential.

What interests me for our present purpose is that 'sort of mix' which occurs. Note the momentary hesitation, the uncertainty, the challenge, before we decide on a course of action or inaction. Note the slight uncertainty, even embarrassment, possibly the excitement, even euphoria, as we approach from a distance. I have caught sight of you and cam momentarily 'thrown'. You now catch sight of me and find yourself adjusting, ordering and settling a momentary confusion.

Can anything be more important than how we are prior to such a peremptory meeting? I would not wish to be unprepared, for fear of making an inexpedient move. This is understandable only because I know how much I stand to gain by making the right move, even a good move. What I would wish to have at hand is that 'unfailing sensibility' I mentioned a while ago, that openness underpinned by awareness, specifically by that awareness of mood in myself, because this amounts to nothing less than a creative channel for your sake. My awareness of mood in myself is not a consciousness of my mood, let's just remind ourselves of that. If I happen to be grouchy or full of myself when we meet, that is unfortunate. In that case I am ill prepared. If you too are grouchy or full of yourself, our two moods will probably cause us to bounce off each other like things, like billiard balls. Of course it helps if I am at least conscious of my mood. Conscience may come to my aid just in good time.

15

What I would prefer however is an awareness of mood in myself, because then, as we meet, that unfailing sensibility kicks in, in response to your mood – of depression or elation. If it should happen that you too are prepared and aware of mood in yourself, then really there is no need for that sensibility in me.

The sensibility I mean allows me readily to suffer your mood at that time, given that it exists. There will be little or no reaction in me to your depressive or elative state but there will be an immediate, or almost immediate, alleviation or grounding of your state.

Moods separate us. They have to be overcome in some way if we are to communicate. Communication towards communion implies a 'working up' of our moods. But mood does not separate us. It is the platform on which we may usefully conjoin.

Also worth considering is that my business is not to argue with your moods, to challenge or criticize them, but to become, and remain, and become again – aware of mood in myself. It is not 'my' mood but mood in myself. It does not exist except as I am aware of it – along with outward reality.

That 'unfailing sensibility' which springs at the right moment from my objective mood awareness accounts for any proportionate degree of confidence I have in the company of others because I can do more than just 'get on' with them, socially. Such a 'getting on', to which we refer as socializing, is at bottom a stale and stagnant affair and any potentially creative person will shun 'society' if he fears he cannot come up with sufficient awareness. And of course he would be smart to do so. In the end we are wise simply to walkway, not impolitely if possible, from anyone who insists on his conscious moods with such an unconscientious intensity and forcefulness that however much we wish we could, we simply can no longer cope. But that would amount to an honest admission of our own limitations and must not contain resentment or condemnation.

Exclusively in terms of consciousness we will never get over the apparent contradiction that mood in myself is the same as my awareness of mood in myself. Conscientiously it will at least reveal itself as a problem that may be solved. Exclusively conscious objectivity, for one thing, applies to outside phenomena. Such phenomena are meaningless to our awareness, which allows us to acknowledge and accredit inward and outward reality. There is no meeting-ground for those who insist on their consciousness and those who choose to be aware. Not that the latter are unconscious but that the former are unaware.

*

Depression and elation, we have said, are not moods but mood. We cannot be in a mood of depression, a depressed mood, or in an elated mood. All the same, if I am depressed, that is to say if this strikes me at the moment as an apt description of how I am, and of my 'state of being', then why not put it to the test? If it's not a mood, then I'm quite happy to continue like that and carry on regardless. I am content to be depressed if this depression is mood and not a mood, a state of being. Similarly I will be quite happy and content – at peace, let us say – to be elated and to continue being and working, if this elation is not a state of being, not a mood. Elation as a mood or state of being implies a degree of restlessness, just as depression as a mood implies a lack of peace. We can use our knowledge of peace and rest to test whether we are in a mood or not.

So let's be practical. The bottom line is that we don't want to get overwhelmed or carried away, by moods. Being depressed or elated is in itself quite normal. It implies the challenge we expect and welcome as our next task, our next introduction to a piece of work. Only the dead move about in a steady state of non-thinking and non-feeling and they are bound to interpret every vestige or inkling of life as the onset of the great catastrophe. By doing so they then actually bring it onto themselves.

17

However our god is the god of the living, so it is the living who concern us.

It is normal to be in peace and at rest, to be depressed or elated, because it is normal to be at some task, to be working, to be doing something. Even just plain being has to be included here. For many on the earth today practical being is downright impossible, for reasons too numerous to mention here. But then being, good and proper, is not just a case of idly hanging around. Being is not being dead. It is living in its primitive occupation and manifestation. Being itself is organic. We can intend to be and do so. Therefore depression or elation, as we use those terms here, are part of the equation. Our mystical approach to god, for example, implies that we are either depressed or elated by god.

Whatever words or concepts we agree to use for the sake of this conversation, the point I want to make is that the distinction between mood and moods is not cut and dried in practice. At this moment my knee and elbow joints hurt and if I'm not careful this will put me in a bad mood, which in turn will bias my working point of view. I will see enemies where there are none. I will make enemies of my knees and elbows, which is no way to make the pain go away and certainly no way to make my joints better.

Perhaps we should distinguish between being depressed and being in a depression, even as we distinguish between suffering and being in pain.

Even the way I think of my painful joints as 'putting me in a bad mood' is already an invitation to a depressive mood. If I end up in a bad mood it won't be because of the pain in my joints but on account of a lack of awareness, including consciousness and conscience. Always and again here too I need to assume the responsibility if I am to continue in, or return to, the sweet order of reality rather than colluding in the falsification of my human nature; also assuming the responsibility does not imply a Luciferian self-will to rule the roost. Neither does it

18

mean, in the strict sense, that if anyone is to blame, I am. Neither the victor nor the victim need to be invited into the relation.

What I do know, and what I count on, is that my soul, perceived as mood, guarantees my wholeness, my wholeness not as an individual, consumed by an idea of perfection, but as a growing and working human being. My soul is not inert and absent, not forgotten or discredited, but present and organic. My soul is good and with me, on my side and perfectly available. Not only is it my portion of god but it is also my interpreter of god, so naturally I want to keep in touch with it. Moods, by comparison, good or bad, are like barriers I erect, or like thickets I allow to grow, between myself and my soul. Thee hindrances are therefore not good and I would refer to them not as soul but psyche.

Never forget that elation, too, can turn into a mood. You meet someone you have looked forward to meting. You get excited. You say things you afterwards wish you hadn't said. The euphoric mood can be the worst offender because we confuse energy with life. We suppose more life means more enthusiasm, more high spirits, being in love. But being in love is not loving, just like being in pain is not suffering. And energy is not life. Once you have experienced normal bliss you shun ecstasy. Normally we would shun all states, pleasant or unpleasant – those of us who want to get ahead and make a real contribution.

*

Soul is infused, we have no choice about that. Of course we are at liberty to ignore this, to deny it, to make something out of it so that we can take cheap credit for it and increase our might-ratio. All of that, however, has to be undone eventually if we are to understand the soul-principle in ourselves as infused god-head. What we can know, in practical terms, of our own soul, not as speculation but as experience, is either mood or dream. We may know our soul objectively or subjectively

19

and this is a great consolation because the object and the subject are the two sides of our existence, so we need never fear the loss of our soul except through our own abuse of neglect.

Soul is always infused, we cannot imagine it otherwise. When I speak of my own soul I refer to that aspect of infused soul of which I am aware as mood or dream. Those who picture 'the soul' as a thing will argue about the time when an individual is endowed with this thing, before birth or after birth or maybe after a visit to some church. However there is god, the good spirit of merciful love and there is god's constant and continuing influence on us, and we are aware of this influence as our soul. It is not a thing, an abstract entity or theological idea but good spirit experienced in the particular within us. We experience it objectively as mood, as depression or elation of which we are aware, or subjectively as dream, as images or symbols which we perceive.

\*

We turn now to our soul subjectively encountered as dream.

Here too we have to distinguish between dream and dreams. We speak of dreams as we do of moods and perhaps they fascinate us. Certainly they draw us away from the light of day, which we do not know at such a time and we can become quite infatuated by our dreams, as they complicate our existence and influence our behaviour. Any interest we take in them however does not bring us into closer proximity to our operational soul. The images and symbols which do cross our path however, often in a startlingly realistic fashion, do give rise to imagination as a faculty which at first merely pictures whatever comes its way. This rudimentary and indistinct imagination can hardly be said to be ours, since it drugs us or drives us in turns and not at all as we can control or predict.

Images and symbols are not necessarily dreams but they may be. Or rather let's put it this way: In the beginning we are caught up in a great welter of symbols and images. Symbols and images differ in terms of meaning. An image conceals relevant meaning while a symbol reveals irrelevant meaning. The relevance and the irrelevance are to me or to you as a potential person. An individual is caught up in, or intrigued by, images and symbols so that he will become a person instead. In order to understand this we have to remember that an individual is not a person but rather someone who is engrossed in or produced by his individuality so that the natural progress to personhood is hindered or interrupted. Individuals therefore must in a certain sense take a step or two backwards before they can advance human naturally to personhood and this of course they are not readily willing to do. As an individual I am captivated to an extent by an ego and I derive pleasure from a degree of selfishness in being or behaviour. I am also acquainted with pain due to the futile struggle for meaning that accompanies all selfishness. Sooner or later this struggle becomes the paramount theme and feature of my existence.

Out of this struggle a rudimentary imagination is born. Representation would be a better word for it. We take pains to represent the symbols and images we come across in an effort to extract from them relevant meaning because we dimly sense the importance of such meaning if we are ever to advance to personhood in community rather than remaining stuck as individuals in society.

The representation of images and symbols is, however, a most peculiar business indeed. Our problem is that we see symbols and images everywhere. The world around us and also our psyche are a welter of images and symbols. We do not stand back from them and observe them with equanimity but we are problematically involved with them. We are even to ourselves in turns an image, concealing relevant meaning or a symbol, revealing irrelevant meaning. The task we set ourselves, to discover and own for ourselves relevant meaning by way of representation, seems to get us closer and closer to our goal but we never quite get there. Just as we are about to grasp the reward we are drugged, our hopes are once again dashed, and no sooner does it occur to us to give up than we are once again driven into the fray, as if our salvation depended on it. So we make a thing out of the struggle, for the sake of reputation and fame. What we do not come up with is truly relevant meaning, for the world and for ourselves, but this does not prevent us from making quite a stir. Quite possibly we help people by drugging those who are driven and driving those who are drugged, so that the process of *enantiodromia* acts itself out here too, dramatically in the public realm and pathetically in the private sphere.

Perception at this stage does not play a role. Representation, as a consequence, may become something like the magic potion of the mountebank, the supposed panacea of the quack, the cult of the religious maniac.

If this rudimentary, merely representational imagination is not to get out of hand, to the point where many are stirred up to harmful foolishness or misled into the spiritual doldrums, presentation must take over from representation. Where representation tends to become automatic and mechanical, presentation presupposes a degree of quality, not just quantity, which in turn calls for honesty and humility.

When we present images and symbols we participate in an act of transformation which does make relevant meaning accessible. No longer do we merely react to phenomena, as if that could satisfy or create a purpose. Images and symbols, as we present them, no longer masquerade as things in themselves but now we see them as things which are willing to be transformed, thereby losing their problematic character and also of course their contradictory appeal. Our task has become much more of an inward occupation because honesty and humility are involved, where previously a kind of duplicity always held sway, which readily gave rise to excesses and infractions.

As soon as we present a symbol or an image, our imagination becomes to that extent distinct. We become capable of imagining the world and ourselves as meaningful. Things come true as beings. We begin to make contact with our soul as dream.

*

Our representation of symbols and images, which we could as readily call appearances at this stage, is not intentional but quite automatic. If we did not represent them, we would, after a short time, be thoroughly disoriented and deluded. So it comes as no surprise that what we experience of the world and of ourselves at this low ebb of our existence barely deserves the name of experience because we are like someone who is driven into himself by a shock and then his equilibrium re-establishes itself so that he ends up unchanged, exactly as he was before that shock. Appearances occur as trivialities and are not genuinely known.

Representation happens and we are lucky that it does. At this lowest stage of our existence, when we are only, so to speak, ticking over and making time, the various beings which surround us and of which we ourselves, after all, are one, are not available to us as beings but only as things and mostly only as the surface of things. We see only the shadows of beings and our seeing is representational, like an echo which sounds in us and we notice it but take no account of it. We exist in a shadow world and we ourselves are shadows.

One might speak of it as a kind of stalemate, once we have sunk this low. All it takes is sufficient neglect and miseducation. Children, as a rule, are wonderfully at home in the world and in themselves but they need to be brought up and that is where so much is neglected. Then, when the results of a poor upbringing manifest themselves, education should be supplied as the remedy but all too often accounts to nothing more than a conscious distortion and aggravation of the confused and deluded child. The child or young individual is literally taught to

23

represent appearances. What kind of a teaching is it, which makes a virtue of, and attaches merit and reward to, that which would otherwise happen in any case, as an emergent reflex? The thoughtless and uncreative manipulation and control of insignificant data is represented institutionally as a necessary and culturally progressive step in the direction of social stature and personal maturity. A safety feature and emergency measure of our human nature, the representation of imagined and symbolic 'mere appearances' at a time when creative knowing has been cast aside, is turned into the criterion of attainment on which something called civilization is made to depend. A child stumbles and falls and instead of helping him up and maybe showing him how to be more careful, we trip him up again and again until he can vouch for the fact that the ground is solid and does not swallow him, something which would very likely never have occurred to him otherwise but now he is patted on the head for this insight.

Children, due to insufficient upbringing and miseducation, turn into immature adults who are suddenly faced with the predicament of irresponsibility and inauthenticity when confronted by images and symbols which point to each one of them individually in the most singular and peculiar fashion. The experience of being singled out as a lonely individual visits the immature adult, who still merely and largely represents what he comes across, so that he not only wonders but he is forced to wonder about the why and wherefore of this experience.

Even this anxiety can for a while be represented. However the crisis looms. No on can say ahead of time at which point presentation will become possible, neither in himself nor in another. Honesty and humility must be intentional, they cannot just happen, like representation. It occurs to us, perhaps overnight, that we may after all be capable of a beneficial input into our existence, in terms of or welfare. The only difference we made in appearances until now are between those we like and those we do not like, between those which please and those

24

which displease us. The fact that those which at first pleased us all too soon disappointed us and that those which initially displeased us seemed somehow more interesting, carried not much significance for us. What we liked soon paled and what we disliked stimulated but those were just more accidents for us and explanations annoyed us. We prided ourselves on our spontaneity which was essentially our taking liberties with the mercy of god. This mercy sustains us for a time, no one can say for how long. At a definite and decisive point in our life, it is slightly removed, or rather it recedes, we stray away even from it – and then the panic sets in. This is a truly educational moment. The lack of meaning in our world and our own insignificance hits us between the eyes. How fortunate if someone who is near us can set us an example of what we would be well and wise to do now, which we can and do accept.

What we really need is an example of honesty and humility. A living example of this can work wonders. We are suddenly and momentarily released from our servitude to chance and accident, so that we truly imagine and perceive. What we imagine might be described as a world of totally interconnected beings and I myself as a whole being perfectly at home in it.

Such an image, or images, are highly significant for us and fraught with meaning. We feel quite transformed by them. Presence of mind might allow us to compare this for once real experience to our childhood, when we were still content to be left alone at times in our peaceful, natural surroundings.

Not only do we imagine but we also perceive. What we perceive is a definite opportunity for perfection and welfare. It occurs to us that yes, something somehow can be done by us so that significance and meaning may become our stock in trade. At the same time it may occur to us how long we have been blithely sailing before a borrowed wind. We had blindly relied on fate and suddenly fate is no longer reliable and our eyes are opened – for a moment.

25

Neither the glorious imagination nor the encouraging perception last – nor are they meant to last. They too, still, after all, happened to us. Without that example of honesty and humility we would still be in a panic, clinging to straws or just plain back in our previous state of meaninglessness and insignificance, where the images and symbols of reality just plain don't register.

What matters now is that the exemplary honesty and humility which served us so well is taken up by ourselves. We are in a position similar to the one who has fallen in love and will soon fall out of love again unless he learns to love. The fortuitous occurrence has given us a taste for the bread which we must now learn to bake. And there can be no question that we have what it takes to do the learning, otherwise that experience would not have occurred to us and we would still be stumbling along in slovenly disregard of our human nature and stature.

What we have to look at now therefore is this honesty and humility which is to take over from our stupid self-reliance and our ignorant self-satisfaction. Like the one who has fallen in love we have fallen into honesty and humility. This has given us a taste for what we might achieve. Perhaps we have to experience a few times what it feels like, if we rest on our undeserved laurels. How painfully bitter are the fruits of disingenuousness and presumptuousness now! Our senses become increasingly keen to a greater power that means us well.

\*

How is dream subjective? How is imagery and symbol subjective? We need to make this clear. Images and symbols do not an longer, or not yet, belong to the twin realm of imagination and perception because they appeal and occur to us as isolated cases. They are not dream but dreams. Each one could be called a separate dream and we represent a collection of them. Each one either conceals relevant meaning or reveals irrelevant meaning. We strive to discover what is concealed and to make relevant what is revealed and this goes as much for our experience, loosely speaking, when we sleep as when we wake. It has long been recognized that when we sleep we may experience two kinds of dreams. One is imagined, the other symbolic. The one that is imagined is, however of the imaginative calibre which we called representational. So let us simply stick with the fact that all particular images and symbols are representational and not presented or present. For the purpose of our study we call them all dreams, whether we come across them during sleep or while we are awake. Not that those who neither perceive nor truly and distinctly imagine would thank us for describing what they do in their approach to the world and themselves as dreaming but we nonetheless have a good reason for doing so. We want to distinguish this representational existence from one that is present, where the world and oneself is presented and therefore transformed. We would like to arrive at the point where perception and imagination become possible for us intentionally, due to our honest predisposition and our humble disposition, and then we will live in the world for which we are created and which is created for us. Nothing less than such a communality of being will satisfy us. The community of beings is our aim. Therefore we subject ourselves to the greater power that means us well. Meanwhile we present our dream, the subjective aspect of our soul.

The honest and humble presentation of image and symbol is intentional. We present what we experience – what is present to us – as dream. We present it perceptively and imaginatively. Not a chance of heedless happiness or of disappointment and confusion now. Ignorance and stupidity are shut out as we perform a meaningful and relevant task.

*

To dream does not mean right away to sleep. At the moment, for example, I am dreaming in the sense that I am in touch with that aspect of my soul. It's an unusual way of talking about it but let's see how far it gets us. I am looking at the phenomenon of dream from the point of view of perception and imagination, so that images and symbols are transformed right away into relevant meaning. The smooth transition from dream into relevant meaning implies a high degree of practical energy and application of course. Commonly one would take no pains to distinguish especially between mood and dream but for the sake of knowledge and understanding I emphasize dream now just as previously we concentrated on mood. One of these is not more important than the other but at times one prevails over the other. Or perhaps we should say that either mood precedes or dream prevails. The left and the right hand consciousness-operate. We are reminded of how either the will predominates or the intellect preponders but either one at a time in the absence of the other does not work. When we study what the left hand is especially good at, we do not mean to suggest that it can do anything useful in isolation. So much for the metaphor of the two hands.

Where dream prevails we can expect an emphasis on image and symbol. Image draws us into the unique nature of an given phenomenon and unites us with its being. We become especially cognizant of how this phenomenon is like nothing else and this insight reminds us how we too are singular and unique and therefore special. The phenomenon may be a leaf on a tree, a person we know or even some historically documented event. The leaf is not an image, nor do we produce an image of the leaf; that has to do with representation, when our imagination is not yet, or no longer, a distinct faculty for which we have taken honest responsibility. We are not asking here what is an image but what is image; not what is a symbol but what is symbol. Our recognition of dream as one operational aspect of our soul (akin to body rather than to mind) demands that we accredit the initial experience of dream, the dreaming which we subjectively know as we do it, and that we do not confound this with any

dream that has merely happened to us, when distinct imagination and true perception were not in play

Image, then, like symbol, is known to us because we have
decided to co-operate with our dream soul; there is no way that
image or symbol can occur to us, accidentally. What occurs to us
like that are dreams, images and symbols. Those who begin with
dreams, with images and symbols or with dreams as images
and symbols and undertake to construct a collective reality
from this, can only end up with more images and symbols, on
which they will of course have pressed their own individual
stamp. The life we find is not the life that lasts.

Our soul as dream is ever present, like our soul as mood.
We know our dream soul in terms of image and symbol, just as
we experience our mood soul in terms of depression and elation. What counts is that we begin with intentional, not with
haphazard knowledge and experience. It is our volition and intention that carries our human-natural privilege and birthright
into the equation, so that we may come up, not with yet another
multiplicity of temporal states, adding to the one-thousand and
one things so that there shall be two-thousand and two, but
with a contemporary contribution to significant and meaningful
order, in the interest of a greater abundance of eternal life.

*

Image and symbol are what turns up and turns out for us
not while we are asleep, or in a state of semi-consciousness as
can happen all too readily when we join forces all too indul-
gently with those who have fallen asleep with their eyes open,
but when we honestly and humbly subject ourselves to the one
who is benevolently greater than we are and willing to inform
us in terms of our dream soul. Dream soul and mood soul are
doctrine but image and symbol, like depression and elation, are
experience. I call it living, or live, doctrine because it is arrived
at through living experience, not with one hand on the public
certificate and the other on the money belt. It would be helpful

29

if one could make this experience more creditable and more accessible because that would be one way of curing the modern miasma for those few who wish to be cured. Cure in this case is not the establishment of a collective facility (or a facile collectivity) for rendering moods and dreams magically exciting and mythically interesting. It has nothing to do with gatherings of the like-minded for the sake of cultic or esoteric prestige. People will gather to support whatever seems to justify their gathering. The collectivity is what counts for them, even if only in the name of a spurious individuation and differentiation. As one 'church' decays another takes over.

No, cure in this case simply means the empowerment of an individual person in community. It means the successful upbringing of children and the maturity of men and women, in a world that is not mistaken but appreciated and on the earth for which we take a caring responsibility.

\*

The subjective experience of image takes us into that realm of ourselves where we know the reality to come, so that we may share it with the members of our community and with the family of man. The subjective experience of symbol, by comparison, allows us to interpret the world around us in such a way that its being as world becomes sensibly manifest. Dream as image therefore locates for us all those contemporary shortfalls in human beings as we have known and loved them and supplies us with ample remedy. As we have partaken in the past of imperfection, so we are supplied with the means of perfection – in our work. Dream can only make sense to the working human being. Only what we pass on is revealed to us, so that discovery and disclosure go hand in hand.

Symbol means world interpretation. World is innumerable beings but the world is a number of things. When things come true, having been interpreted, they end up as beings. In that sense the interpreted world is world. Therefore we say that world without end is our dream come true.

Images and symbols assail us. How can it be otherwise than that we, as working human beings, are exposed to the world and to things? Images stimulate our imagination, symbols appeal to our perception. We go on a journey, we meet people, we read books. Images conceal relevant meaning. Our imagination is stimulated. What are we to do? We rely on wisdom to see us through. We fall back on wisdom, which teaches us that our stimulated imagination cannot penetrate the irrelevant meaning of images. Our perception cannot reveal the meaning of symbols. Nonetheless it is important that our imagination, where there was none or where it had decayed, is stimulated and that our perception, where it exists no longer or not yet, is appealed to. Anxiety and stress ensue, which we may recognize. We are anxious for ourselves and anxious for those around us. Stressful situations abound. If we are fortunate we will have fellowship with one who is wise. Wisdom will 'rub off' on us. We depend as much on this wisdom to see us through the time of anxiety and stress in the face of images and symbols, as our imagination and perception develop, as we then depend on an example of humility and honesty to teach us how to subject ourselves to image and symbol, that is: to dream.

*

Wisdom neutralizes images and symbols. Meanwhile our imagination and perception have been quickened. Wisdom makes plain for us the redundancy of image and symbol representation. Why should we adopt an image as, say, a learning device if we cannot even agree on its outline, not to mention its effective content? Take God as an image. Now ask the next twenty people what they mean by God and then try to find a common denominator – given that those people have said what they really believe, feel and think. God as an image is no closer to us than an image of the present prime minister of England or of Napo-

31

leon Bonaparte. A representation of this God image merely stresses its existential impossibilities, as theologians have demonstrated through the ages. When a mystic pleads with god to rid him of God, he wants rid of the image representations which block his view of god as image, ever present.

Artists 'create' images. Strictly speaking these are representations of something that has moved them presently and they know not what but they present it again. This 'again' gives the game away. The art worker knows what he does, the artist does not. The artist makes a thing out of that which would be a being. There is a world of difference.

Representations allow us to point the finger at something and call it 'bad' or 'good', meaning we like it, it is like ourselves, or we do not like it, it is not like ourselves. Critics thrive on representations.

The concealed relevant meaning of an image is bound to intrigue us. Consider how this meaning is concealed in the first place. I absentmindedly look at a tree, because it is there, for no other reason, or because I don't want to bump into it. Many times I have looked at it and then managed to walk around it. This time something about it touches me – where I am not used to being touched and where I am therefore afraid of being touched. So reactively I shut the tree out. I deaden in myself what has sprung into life upon being touched. The tree itself hasn't a clue what this is about. The tree is a being gloriously in itself. Whether or not it wishes I had entrusted it with a short communication, a human response, that is another story. For the moment I want to look only at what goes on in terms of the human being who has been inwardly moved by the being of the tree and has reacted negatively, in denial. He has struck back like someone who has been hurt and reacts automatically. "What? You say we want to kill you? How do you arrive at that conclusion?" – said those who had been reminded by that Jesus who is revered by the Christians that they wanted to kill him just because he lived and existed in such a way that they could not help but be moved inwardly where they had never been moved. Of course he had made it his task to bring human being to the fore. The one who is reminded unusually by our tree of his inwardness is simply moved by the being of that tree, by the fact that this tree is, which until then he had ignored and had been allowed to ignore. By killing off the tree emotion in himself he changes the tree into an image – for himself.

This could be called a subjective reflex. He does not subject himself to anyone or anything however but he subjects the tree to himself, which is not a healthy move. That tree will never again be just another tree for him. In a sense it will haunt him. More accurately, he will feel haunted by it. The tree  itself probably hasn't even noticed him.

When he kills the tree emotion in himself he rejects the tree as it momentarily became for him and unconsciously he decides he want it back the way it used to be, just another thing among a thousand and one things. He re-presents the tree. It's as if he were saying: "Look, stop pretending you are extraordinary, individual, singular, peculiar and unique. I don't wish to know that and besides it isn't true. That little emotional accident I just had shall be wiped from the surface of the earth so that in spite of your stimulating and appealing being there for a moment I re-delegate you to the realm of extinction, outside myself, a thing among things like myself. You must understand that I don't like to be reminded of my thing-status; it hurts, I'm sorry."

I'm getting a little bit apologetic there and that is actually part of the image experience. The other part is: "How dare you do this to me! I was perfectly happy as a thing, a least so it seems to me now, in comparison to this resentment you have made me feel!"

The other part is the accusatory mood. "You have made me feel bad. I hate you." Sound familiar? The accusation, mind you, is mixed with guilt, just as the apology is mixed with shame. Honesty and humility do not play a role in either case however. What remains is a perplexity, a sense of intrigue: "What is it that came over me? I can't quite accept that the tree was to blame. However I'll not trust the image of that tree in future."

It is I who have made myself responsible for that image. Neither by way of imagination nor perception can I work out the meaning of it. I remain perplexed, mistrustful, self-conscious in terms of it.

Wisdom comes to my aid. My imagination becomes distinct. My perception comes true. The image is neutralized. I am willing to take another look at that tree as the singular being that it is – and as the singular being that I am.

*

Simply to present what we have experienced, this is not the same as representing it. It appears that we ourselves are responsible if our experience amounts to images and symbols. Symbols reveal irrelevant meaning and this leads us astray because we are so hungry for meaning, for sense, that the lack of relevance does not immediately occur to us.

How wonderful to have a body of knowledge! If perchance it should die, we soon experience its resurrection. I wonder how we have learned to be so confident. A body is sense and meaning, is purpose and even value. Disembodied I become a nuisance to the gods and a danger to myself, hence the strenuous search for sense and meaning at times.

It might be quite interesting to find out how symbols are brought about; how they are coaxed into existence, really by our self-love. We have discovered that our self rewards us with a little pleasure if we defer to it at such moments as when we are caught up in a dispute between what we would like to do and what we ought to do. Instead of hating our self and settling the dispute we come to a duplicitous arrangement with that problematic experience. We say: Look, I will give you some play room if you promise to stay out of my hair. I will trust you but only as far as I can throw you. If I pretend you are real, you must agree to pretend you are relevant.

This does in fact work for a while. The problem appears to be solved on account of the way we look at the thing. Understandably we cultivate that look. There are so many problems and so few solutions! We actually believe that problems come our way unbidden and underserved. One symbol after another is cultivated, always in the hope that we continue to have the choice to reject the contradiction of pleasure and duty by setting up this compromise with our self, which will not, because it cannot, do good. We do not end up with an intriguing thing, as in the case of an image, but with irresolution and trivial circumstances. Surely this is true, it must be true, we think, but even if it is, what has that to do with me?

It has nothing to do with us because we distanced ourselves from the reality of it at the start, when that reality first confronted us. We did that without knowing, of course. Now when we realize what we have ended up with, we are troubled in our mind and we begin to think: How could I appropriate meaning and sense for myself? Not by taking thought however can we overcome those troubles. After all, the symbolism, while it challenges our mind, stems initially from our unreflective mind and this, you might say, has damaged it at the root. Once again, with the advent of consciousness also comes consciousness of shortfall.

Wisdom neutralizes the symbol, creates a breathing space. Honestly and humbly we are now able to view the world and ourselves, to put it as simply as possible, as uncontradictory and unproblematic flesh and blood, and this is symbolic, without being a symbol.

*

35

Why are we so hungry for meaning? Why is it so important for us that the world should make sense?

The thirst for knowledge is an all-consuming thirst and if we cannot find real knowledge we stoop to substitutes. Images and symbols, of our own creation, are such substitutes. We decline the real food that comes our way and then try to thrive on the fruits of our rejection. The real food is so strange and foreign to us that it hurts to have it presented to us. Is it any wonder that we reject it? Would it be much use to speculate why it hurts? Better by far to learn wisdom.

We can relearn wisdom. Once we were wise, when we were children. At that time we didn't know it. Now our thirst for knowledge is such that we would even know how it was that we were wise once. Then we would know what it means to be wise. Then we would be wise. Images and symbols would no longer exercise their hold over us. The political rally, the advertising campaign, the pop concert: good fun, but meaningless. Not to be touched by the accidental products of our own unreadiness for influential reality is a great step forward. Not that we should harden our hearts, for that is sheer foolishness but that we should learn to step back inwardly from the welter of opinion and emotion that is popular, public and political – that is the beginning of wisdom.

Imagine yourself as a child. You are cheerful by instinct. Your trust in the material earth is unquestioning. The starry universe fills you with wonder. The cloudy sky is an ever changing panorama for you and your own inwardness changes along with it. You are joyful, reflective, peacefully involved in what takes your interest. It wouldn't occur to you to argue with any sensation or to cling to it for any reason under the sun. Pleasure comes and goes and you naturally respect its lawfulness. You are open to the day as to a well-written book, the author of which you trust.

The most telling circumstance is that you are inwardly at home – albeit without knowing it. It would not occur to you that things might be otherwise. Calling this a circumstance is in no way off the mark since your inward disposition shapes your world. You know fine well that the world is hell to one man and heaven to another. During your childhood, consciousness at times assailed you to the accompaniment of pain. Then your inwardness occurred to you momentarily as somehow separate from, as different from, outward reality. Eventually these moments of painful consciousness would occur more frequently and less intensely. You were brought up not to blame anyone but to forgive, not to seek revenge but to endure. You saw examples around you of patient endurance, of the courageous willingness to stand alone. This deepened your appreciation of an inward landscape while outward reality became increasingly benign.

In your childlike wisdom you imbibed consciousness and became more knowledgeable. The stream of wisdom was not dammed, not interrupted, you merely learned to step in and out of it, as the one who knows he does and is done to. The fact that your doing at first met with opposition did not greatly surprise you. You had been taught by wise teachers to expect as much. You had been taught honesty and humility. Doing nevertheless, this was what counted. The energetic careers of those who loved their selves and swam in a pool of symbols and images seemed fascinating but not worthy of imitation, for you were learning that by hating your self, that self which so often reared up between yourself and your wisdom, you were able to accumulate sound sense and to gain relevant meaning. This was more important for you than that external fitness for survival which dominated as the spirit of the times. In fact it was so important for you that you concealed your preference and remained mindful of the irrelevance of acted out consciousness without criticizing it.

On the surface it would seem impossible to give preference to an idea of what we mean by dream and mood. And yet should we not attempt to unite these two concepts in a single one without necessarily forcing experience to follow suit? Indeed depression and elation sum up an abundance of experience on the side of mood, very much comparable, as we have seen, to image and symbol on the side of dream. The latter is ours subjectively, the former is objective. Images, symbols, depressions and elations we leave out of consideration now, although of course here too we are all too well aware of how much accidental existence is implied by these four meagre references.

We have taken note, perhaps insufficiently, of the experience, objective and subjective, of mood and dream as depression and elation and as image and symbol, as distinct from mood and dream as doctrinal elements. If I examine myself I may or may not find myself in a mood or in a dream. I may or may not find myself beset by a depression or an elation. If not, then I am free to approach my soul, because my hands, so to speak, are clean. I may begin to do work now that goes beyond the effect of cleansing and healing. If I describe this work as cooperative with my soul, with my soul as objective mood or subjective dream, I imply that my soul is somehow effective and influential.

My soul cooperates with me as long as I give the lead. Awareness of my soul, of myself being truly whole and sound within myself and human-naturally embedded in god, so to speak, allows me to work in this cooperative fashion, which brings forth fruit perfect and singular.

The cooperative effectiveness of my soul I call ideal. As we concentrate our attention on this ideal effectiveness we are bound to come to the conclusion that nothing so much works for us as our infused and now also infusing, soul. It becomes impossible to distinguish between subject and object. We gain nothing by trying to do so. Our distinct imagination lends itself readily to the task of keeping the door open to ideal influence. What all too readily closes the door is indistinct, picturing imagination, which will, however, no longer be a hindrance to us when we have dealt intelligently with our moods and dreams and worked creatively in terms of mood and dream. The practicalities have to be observed and progress, like growth, takes time. For the sake of immediate and eventual recognition we are telescoping, in this study, what in reality may take years to come about and be brought about. The earlier we realize that our own efforts are important and that at the same time efforts are made on our behalf which we must take into account, the better.

The ideal infusion due to our infused soul is into ourselves and into or works, at one and the same time. No such ideal infusion occurs when we do not work. It would not help therefore to have a mistaken conception of work.

The most fitting answer to the question: Why should we work? is: so that we may have life and so that we may have it more abundantly.

But life, as we know, is both personal and communal. You in person and our community, your surroundings and environment both human natural and real, are each distinguishable in themselves but with a view to life they are one. The fact that we cannot cause life but that it is in every conceivable way a gift is underlined by this, but it must be kept in mind when we begin to think in terms of forceful and mechanical cause and effect.

I can work for myself, in which case I become enriched in myself and coincidentally a good example to my community, or I can work first and foremost for my community and for its enrichment, in which case I myself am coincidentally enriched. The enrichment in both cases is gifted life.

The work I do for myself is essential. Unless I have wealth of my own I cannot share it out. I myself, you yourself therefore, will first of all want to take advantage directly of this providential measure which is our infused and infusing soul. Not a part of yourself will gain, not an aspect of yourself, such as a faculty, organ or skill, will be increased but you yourself, if you can imagine that. No greater good is conceivable. It is the good we desire, whatever else we may desire.

*

Mood and dream foreshadow the ideal effectiveness of our soul on behalf of ourselves and others. Really we should say: ...on behalf of ourselves and the family of man, but that would take us too far afield at the moment. Mood and dream indicate for us, each in its own way, that an operational soul is available for us and places in our hands the means whereby we may arrive at, or attain to, this greatest of all benefits within reach of every human being. It makes sense that once we have worked our way through this possibility a few times we will be much less afraid of, and less vulnerable in the presence of, depressions and elations in ourselves and others, while images and symbols, as we accidentally produce them ourselves and as they crop up like weeds all around us, will cause us less anxiety and tempt us less frequently.

*

It seems more than reasonable to question the description of our soul's operational effectiveness as ideal. Surely what we usually mean by an idea stems from the head. So far however there has been no mention of 'an idea', only of an 'ideal' effectiveness and it may be quite possible that this ideality of our soul in some way precedes the occurrence of 'ideas', as we conventionally call them. Once suspects, in fact, that the only explanation for ideas in the head is a misappropriation of our soul's ideality.

40

When we recall how far afield we had to travel and how profoundly we had to search before we cold come to an understanding of our soul's productive originality, this 'capitalism' of ideas will not much surprise us. Is it not as if we had overlooked the spring at its source and were now forced to search for water among the boulders, where we could hear the merry sprinkling and splashing, the gurgling from down below? Now and again we are overjoyed when we come across a trickle in the silt after scratching away the stones and pebbles. What a big thing we make of that!

The ideal does not exist. There is no such thing. How misleading to pretend that there is! Enclosed in our heads we nurse this notion of an ideal originality. Yes, we ourselves are enclosed in our heads, we are playing a game which we take far too seriously. With fearful earnestness we pretend to an achievable perfection which has no connection with our soul. Pride dictates that we persist in this futile endeavour, to the point where we castigate anyone who still mentions a soul and suggests treacherously that the ideal is not achievable. The 'capitalist' position is worth defending, since the only alternative is nihilism and despair. All talk of soul must therefore be condemned outright as wishy-washy sentimentality, as an attack on sound sense and optimistic morality.

This nervous reaction of the 'capitalist' is understandable when we look for a moment a the attempts conventionally made to undermine the head-heavy, or big-headed, approach to an ideal. Once an ideal has been set up and sufficient energy has been invested in it, the conception of soul that seems even credible is that of a disembodied spirituality. We can no longer even imagine such an entity as 'our soul'. The human being as body and soul kept together for the duration is itself 'an idea' and 'the ideal' is permanent duration. The alternative is death, the cessation of happiness, the admission of defeat. One feels culturally obliged at least to pay lip service to this ideal, this

41

central ideal, for the maintenance of which all the other, subsidiary ideals of our civilization are invented. However, as we discovered also during our acquaintance with dreams and moods, every move in a wrong direction is succeeded by a countermove in the opposite wrong direction. 'Soul' as a consequence is set up as a counter-ideal. 'The soul' becomes the myth of the day. This soul cannot be achieved, as the ideal allegedly can, but it must be believed. That is why we call it the myth, with right, because the very act of believing must keep it afloat and before our eyes, otherwise we are counted among the infidel.

The two opposing camps of modern life are thus established: on the right the ideal which must be achieved, on the left the myth which must be believed. Religions hold the ground on the one side, ideologies hold it on the other. Meanwhile religion and ethical action are lost sight of and intentionally ignored.

*

This is all very sad and naturally one wonders what can be done about it. How to get off that nerve-racking, energy-sapping see-saw, that's the question. Should we mock 'soul' and espouse ideology or should we condemn ideology and favour soul? Should we go wrong to the left of to the right? Or perhaps we should just go ahead and blow our brains out.

A fair degree of intelligence is required to arrive at such a deadlock. It is difficult to imagine anything more depressing. In the absence of a way out of the dilemma, one is liable even to deplore the insight which reveals it. It's not however that we have "an eye too many" but that we allow ourselves to be fascinated, infatuated and finally utterly fatigued by that which must seem impossible and at the same time indispensable.

We might step back and ask ourselves how we would offer to assist someone else who finds himself in such a predicament. Must the modern dilemma necessarily end in catastrophe, for the individual as well as for the nation, or are we able to draw on a strength in ourselves which perhaps sidesteps the entire left-right issue and opens an avenue into a plentiful realm of alternatives, all untouched and uncontaminated by myths and ideals?

The illusion of helplessness and the accompanying sensation of being shamefully disheartened need never prevent us from returning, in the fullest awareness, to that intelligence which first revealed to us the dispiriting dilemma and quite simply understanding it, in the light of day as the faculty with which we can courageously complete the task which so far has only half-heartedly been half done.

The suggestion, in other words, is that we actually understand our intelligence rather than only going along with it. By going along with it, by allowing ourselves to be guided by it, we were able to discover how reality separates into two opposing camps, each with its own characteristic images and symbols which either depressed or elated but offered no permanent foot- or handhold. Not only were we not getting anywhere, as modern individuals, but we had run out of ways and means for attacking the problem. Neither by force nor by leniency were we able to accomplish more than a temporary change of appearances. Eventually utter impotence was all that remained.

How can we understand our intelligence? Here we have a faculty which, with practical application, allows us to make dialectic headway. Analysis and synthesis however come to an end as we stand confronted by that deplorable foolishness which is our present state of affairs either idealized or mythified. Only an enthusiastic and sufficiently beguiled audience can sustain us for a short while now before our self-delusion collapses, leaving us being and feeling profoundly inadequate.

In order to understand what is at stake here we have to be willing and able to sustain a very definite shock of enlightenment. The shock is to our self-love, our self-regard and self-respect. Depending on how thoroughly these have been ground down and worn out of us by the torture of the modern predicament, both arrogantly and morbidly, this shock is more or less intense. However we may also have been educated in the right direction, so that we were prepared for what the future was bound to bring and then the shock boils down to recollection, recognition and acknowledgment. All three may be usefully summed up as realization.

*

*Understood intelligence* works as a series of sovereign impulses. We may well have to be driven out of our cultivated minds before we pay heed to such impulses. As children we were guided by them without knowing. Then we were endowed with cultivated minds, by those who meant well but did ill. That was not entirely necessary, or at least not to the extent that it was enforced or for the reasons which were brought forward as sufficient justification. All that was needed was that we should learn how to take the reins of our human nature into our own hands. The passage from youth to maturity requires no more than a modicum of disillusionment, not a programmed, institutionalized world of it. Such a world of disillusion is no longer a passage but a cul-de-sac, like setting up house in the hallway between the front porch and the living-room. The necessary, or rather unavoidable, modicum of disillusion comes about coincidentally in view of those sovereign impulses as presented by mature adults to the young. No one in his right mind would consider even for a moment fastening on those coincidents of disillusion, in order to make something out of them, not to mention the fabrication of orthodox disciplines and universal institutions, on behalf of which benighted souls will give themselves over to destruction.

However not all is doom and gloom. There are among us those who have the courage to speak out and their speech is not one long qualification of half-truths. The willingness to withstand uncertainty and the ability to hold out in the face of the utterly new, these are, of course, prerequisites if we want to take advantage of that inward revolution for which all outside revolutions are evasive excuses.

* * *　　　　　6/9/2004